Brick Math Series

LEARNING SUBTRACTION
USING LEGO® BRICKS

Dr. Shirley Disseler

COMPASS

Learning Subtraction Using LEGO® Bricks — Student Edition

Brigantine Media/Compass Publishing
211 North Avenue
St. Johnsbury, Vermont 05819
Phone: 802-751-8802
Fax: 802-751-8804
E-mail: neil@brigantinemedia.com
Website: www.compasspublishing.org
www.brickmath.com

ORDERING INFORMATION

Quantity sales

Special discounts for schools are available for quantity purchases of physical books and digital downloads. For information, contact Brigantine Media at the address shown above or visit www.brickmath.com.

Individual sales

Brigantine Media/Compass Publishing publications are available through most booksellers. They can also be ordered directly from the publisher.
Phone: 802-751-8802 | Fax: 802-751-8804
www.compasspublishing.org
www.brickmath.com

ISBN 978-1-9384066-8-3

CONTENTS

WHAT DOES IT MEAN TO SUBTRACT?

Part 1

1. Build a model of the number 8 using one 2x4 brick. Build a model of the number 2 by placing two 1x1 bricks or one 1x2 brick to the right of the 2x4 brick, leaving space between the two models. These two models represent the two numbers in a subtraction problem.

The first number is called the _____.

The second number is called the _____.

Draw your models.

2. Model the subtraction of 8 studs – 2 studs by placing the 1x2 brick on top of the 2x4 brick. How many studs are not covered? _____

The uncovered studs show how many are left. This is called the _____.

Draw your model of the solution and label the numbers represented by the bricks.

Write a mathematical statement for your model: _____

3. Make a model of the number 10 using a 1x10 brick. Draw your model.

This model represents the start of a subtraction problem.

Name this number: _____

4. Model the number 3 to the right of your model of 10. This model represents the second part of the subtraction problem. What is the name for this number?

_____

Add your model of 3 to the drawing of your model of 10.

5. Build a model that shows the *difference*.

How many studs of the 1x10 brick are showing after you place the 1x3 brick on top of it?

_____

This means the _____ is 7.

6. Write a mathematical sentence for this problem.

_____

Draw a model that shows the *difference* and label it.

7. Build a different model of the number 10 using bricks other than a 1x10 brick. Build a model to show: 10 studs – 6 studs = ⬜ studs

Share your model with a partner. Draw your model and label each part of the problem. Explain your thinking.

Part 2

1. Can you build a model that shows the number 6 and a model that shows the number 2? Can you build a model that shows the difference between 6 and 2? Draw your model. Label the drawing with subtraction vocabulary words. Write a math sentence for the problem.

2. Can you build a model that shows the number 9 and a model that shows the number 3? Can you build a model that shows the difference between 9 and 3? Draw your model. Label the parts of the drawing and write a math sentence for the problem.

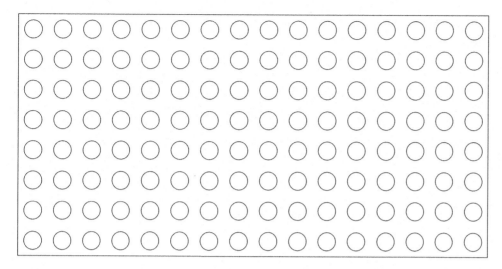

3. Can you build a model for this mathematical sentence? 5 studs – 2 studs = 3 studs

Draw and explain your model in writing. Label all the parts of the model (*minuend, subtrahend, difference*).

4. Can you build a model that shows each part of this math sentence?

8 studs − 4 studs = ☐ studs

Draw and explain your model in writing. Label all the parts of the model (*minuend*, *subtrahend*, *difference*).

_____

_____

_____

Challenge:

Model a subtraction problem with bricks. Do not include the difference in the model. Find a partner and exchange problems. Solve your partner's problem. After you have both completed the problems, discuss your solutions and make sure you can explain both models. Draw both models and your solutions. Write your explanations of both models.

My Problem

_____

_____

_____

Partner's Problem

_____

_____

_____

Assessment:

1. Circle the minuend in the problem: 12 – 5 = 7

2. Circle the subtrahend in the problem: 7 – 5 = 2

3. Circle the difference in the problem: 12 – 7 = 5

4. Build a model that shows a solution to the problem: 8 – 5 = ☐

Draw your model.

5. Build a model of the problem 11 – 3 = 8. Draw your model. Label all the parts of the problem with the correct vocabulary words.

TEN-FRAMES SUBTRACTION WITHIN 20

Part 1

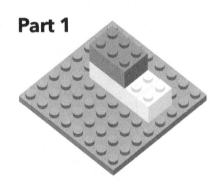

1. Build a ten-frame using bricks of the same color. Build a model of the number 6 on top of the ten-frame with one or more bricks of another color. Count the studs. How many studs are on this model? _____

Draw your model.

2. Build a model of the number 4 on the baseplate with a brick of another color. Draw your model on the baseplate above.

3. Model the subtraction of 4 from 6 by placing the 4 studs on top of the 6 studs. Draw this model on the baseplate above.

4. What is the solution to the problem? _____ *Hint*: The studs that are showing in the middle layer represent the *difference*.

Write a math sentence: _____

Circle the solution in your drawing above.

5. Build a model of the number 12 using two ten-frames.

6. Choose a brick to represent the number 8. Place this brick on the baseplate. Draw your models and write a math sentence.

_____

7. Combine the models to show subtraction by placing the 8 studs on the 12 studs.

Draw this model. How many studs are left over? _____

This number is called the _____.

8. Build a model to show the *difference* between 16 and 12. Start by building two ten-frames. Next, build a model of the number 16 on the ten-frames. Place 12 studs on the same baseplate to show the subtrahend of 12. Combine the two models by placing the 12 studs on top of the 16 studs. Look top down to see how many of the original 16 studs are not covered. What is the *difference*? _____

Draw the models.

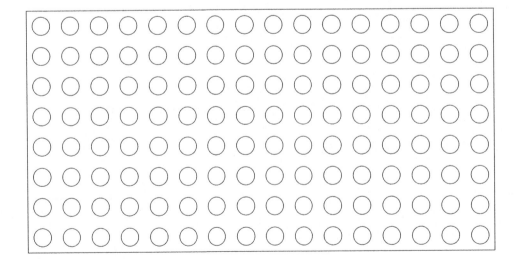

Part 2

1. Can you build two ten-frames and model the subtraction of 12 – 8? Show both sets of numbers. Build another model to show how you found the solution. Draw your models and label all the parts. Write a math sentence for your model.

2. Can you build a ten-frame model of 14 – 5? Show both sets of numbers. Build another model to show how you found the solution. Draw your models and label all the parts. Write a math sentence for your model.

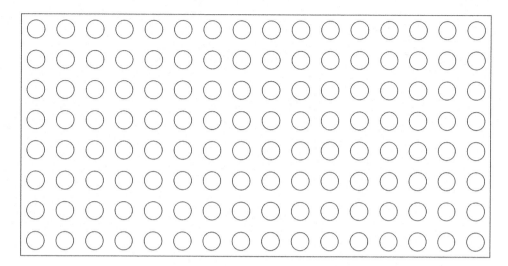

3. Can you build a ten frame model of 20 – 8? Show both sets of numbers. Build another model to show how you found the solution. Draw your models and label all the parts. Write a math sentence for your model.

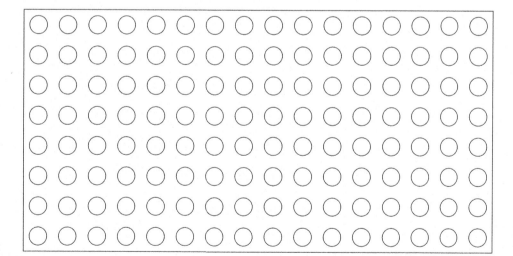

4. Can you build a ten-frame model of 6 – 6? Show both sets of numbers. Build another model to show how you found the solution. Draw your models and label all the parts. Write a math sentence for your model.

Assessment:

1. Make a ten-frame model of 7 – 2. Draw your model. Draw a circle around the *minuend*. Draw a square around the *subtrahend*. What is the *difference*? _____

2. Which brick or bricks represent the *minuend* in this model?

_____

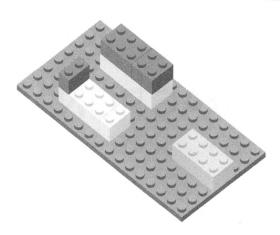

3. Build a ten-frame model of the number 13. Model how to subtract 8 from 13. Draw your solution.

What is the *difference*? _____

```
○ ○ ○ ○ ○ ○ ○ ○ ○ ○ ○ ○ ○ ○
○ ○ ○ ○ ○ ○ ○ ○ ○ ○ ○ ○ ○ ○
○ ○ ○ ○ ○ ○ ○ ○ ○ ○ ○ ○ ○ ○
○ ○ ○ ○ ○ ○ ○ ○ ○ ○ ○ ○ ○ ○
○ ○ ○ ○ ○ ○ ○ ○ ○ ○ ○ ○ ○ ○
○ ○ ○ ○ ○ ○ ○ ○ ○ ○ ○ ○ ○ ○
○ ○ ○ ○ ○ ○ ○ ○ ○ ○ ○ ○ ○ ○
○ ○ ○ ○ ○ ○ ○ ○ ○ ○ ○ ○ ○ ○
```

4. $12 - 7 = 5$

Which number is the *minuend*? _____

Which number is the *difference*? _____

Which number is the *subtrahend*? _____

3

MISSING TERM SUBTRACTION

```
┌─────────────────────────┐
│                         │
│                         │
└─────────────────────────┘
        ┌─────────────────────────┐
──      │                         │
        │                         │
        └─────────────────────────┘
─────────────────────────────────
        ┌─────────────────────────┐
        │                         │
        │                         │
        └─────────────────────────┘
```

Part 1

1. On the diagram, write M, S, or D in the box that shows the correct location of the *minuend*, *subtrahend*, and *difference* in a subtraction problem.

2. Find one 2x6 brick and one 2x2 brick. Draw each brick on the baseplates below. Count the number of studs on each brick and record that number under your drawing of each brick.

_____ studs   _____ studs

3. Place the brick with the larger number of studs on the box above that you labeled *M*. Place the smaller brick on the box labeled *S*.

Discuss with a partner some strategies to find the number that goes in box D. Build a model of your ideas using bricks. Draw your model and explain your strategy.

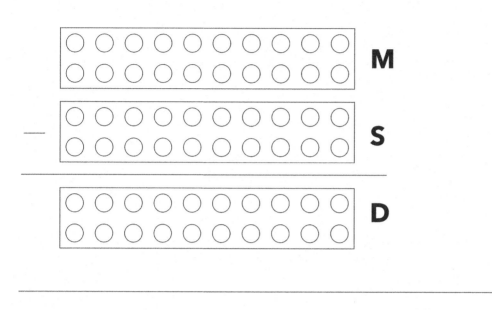

_____

_____

_____

4. Find one 2x4 brick and one 1x2 brick. Draw each brick on the baseplates below. Count the number of studs on each brick and record that number under your drawing of each brick.

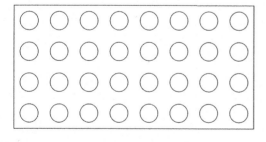

_____ studs   _____studs

5. Place the brick with the largest number of studs on the box labeled M. Place the smaller brick on the box labeled D.

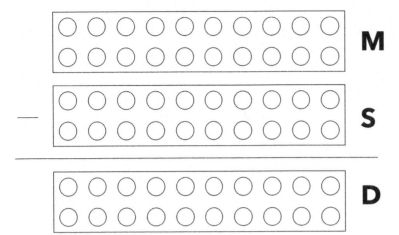

6. Discuss with a partner some strategies to find the number that goes in box S. Build a model of your idea using bricks. Draw your model on the diagram and explain your strategy. Write the math sentence.

_____

_____

_____

7. Find one 2x4 brick and one 1x8 brick. How are these two bricks are alike and different?

_____

_____

_____

Place the 2x4 brick in box S and place the 1x8 brick in box D.

M

S

D

8. What brick goes in Box M? Work with a partner to discuss possible solutions.

9. Build your solution. Draw your solution model above and explain your thinking.

_____

_____

_____

Part 2

1. 6 – 2 = ☐

Choose one brick to show 6 and another brick to show 2.

Draw both bricks and label the number of studs on each brick.

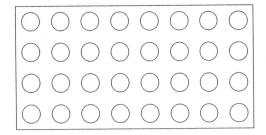 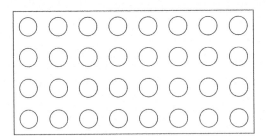

_____ studs   _____ studs

On the diagram of M – S = D, place the 6-stud brick in box M.

On the diagram of M – S = D, place the 2-stud brick in box S.

Find the number that goes in box D and model the solution.

Draw your model and label all the parts of the problem.

Write a math sentence for your model.

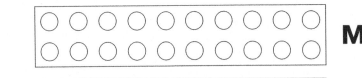 **M**

 **S**

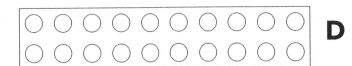 **D**

2. $20 - \boxed{} = 8$

Choose one or more bricks to show 20 and another brick to show 8.

Draw the bricks and label the number of studs on each brick.

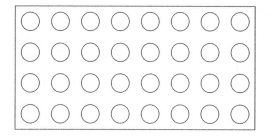   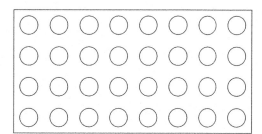

_____ studs   _____studs

On the diagram of M – S = D, place the 20-stud brick or bricks in box M.

On the diagram of M – S = D, place the 8-stud brick in box D.

Find the number that goes in box S and model the solution.

Draw your model and label all the parts of the problem.

Write a math sentence for your model.

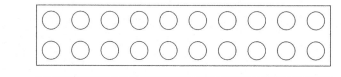 **M**

 **S**

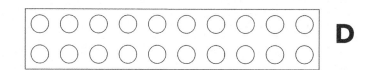 **D**

3. ◻ – 8 = 2

Choose one brick to show 8 and another brick to show 2.

Draw both bricks and label the number of studs on each brick.

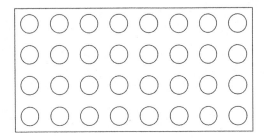   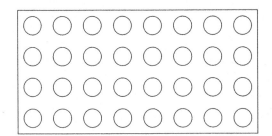

_____ studs   _____studs

On the diagram of M – S = D, place the 8-stud brick in box S.

On the diagram of M – S = D, place the 2-stud brick in box D.

Find the number that goes in box M and model the solution.

Draw your model and label all the parts of the problem.

Write a math sentence for your model.

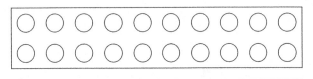 **M**

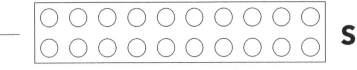 **S**

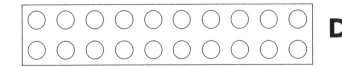 **D**

_____

Challenge:

Model the problem: $20 - 4 - 6 = \boxed{}$

Choose one or more bricks to show 20, another brick to show 4, and another brick to show 6.

Draw all the bricks and label the number of studs on each brick.

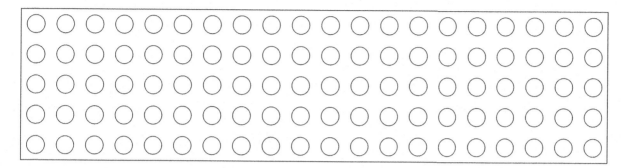

Place the 20-stud brick or bricks in box M.

Place the 4-stud brick in one box S.

Place the 6-stud brick in the other box S.

Find the number that goes in box D and model the solution.

Draw your model and label all the parts of the problem.

Write a math sentence for your model.

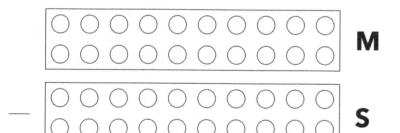 **M**

 **S**

 **S**

D

Assessment:

Use the subtraction diagrams to model the missing part of each subtraction problem. Draw your models.

1. Minuend: 2x6 brick (12 studs)

Subtrahend: 2x4 brick (8 studs)

D is the missing term.

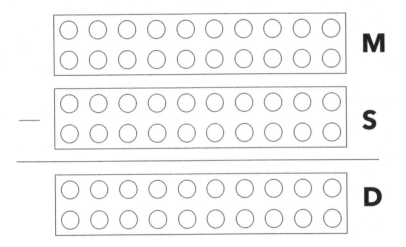

2. Minuend: 2x10 brick (20 studs)

Difference: 2x3 brick (6 studs)

S is the missing term.

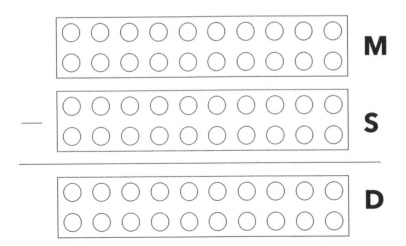

3. Subtrahend: 2x6 brick (12 studs)

Difference: 2x2 brick (4 studs)

M is the missing term.

4. Model the following problem using the subtraction diagram. $10 - 3 - 5 = \boxed{}$

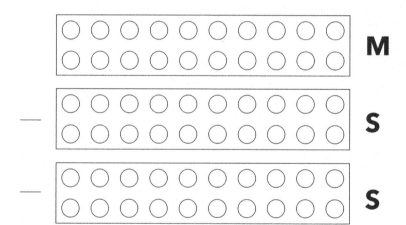

DECOMPOSING NUMBERS / PLACE VALUE

Part 1

1. Build a model for the problem: 22 studs – 8 studs = ☐

Use two 1x10 bricks and one 1x2 brick to show the minuend of 22.

Use one 1x8 brick to show the subtrahend of 8.

2. From the bricks representing 22, decompose one 1x10 brick into ten 1x1 bricks. Add the additional two 1x1 bricks to them to total 12 ones. What do you have now? _____ tens____ones

3. Model the subtraction by placing the 1x8 brick on top of the studs that represent the ones. How many studs are left showing? _____

4. Use more 1x1 bricks to represent the studs left showing. Take the other 1x10 brick that represents the tens and put it next to the 1x1 bricks. How many studs are here? _____

What is the *difference*? _____

5. Draw your model and label it to prove your answer.

6. Build a model for the problem: 33 studs – 16 studs = ☐

Use three 1x10 bricks and one 1x3 brick to show the minuend of 33.

Use one 1x10 brick and one 1x6 brick to show the subtrahend of 16.

Share your model with a partner.

7. Decompose one 1x10 brick and the 1x3 brick from the minuend model into 13 ones.

8. Take the remaining two 1x10 bricks from the minuend model and place them next to the thirteen 1x1 bricks.

9. Take the ten and ones bricks that model the subtrahend and stack them on top of the minuend bricks. How many studs are left over? _____

This term is called the _____.

Part 2

1. Can you build a model to show this math sentence? 26 studs – 19 studs = ☐

Show all the steps, including the decomposing of the tens into ones. How many studs are showing in your solution? _____

Draw the model of your solution. Explain how you found your solution.

_____

_____

_____

2. Can you work with a partner to build a model to show this math sentence?

32 studs – 16 studs = ☐

Show all the steps including the decomposing of the tens.

How many studs are showing in your solution? _____

Draw the model of your solution. Explain how you found your solution.

_____

_____

_____

3. Can you work with a partner to build a model to show this math sentence?

23 studs – 15 studs = ☐

Show all the steps including the decomposing of the tens.

How many studs are showing in your solution? _____

Draw the model of your solution. Explain how you found your solution.

_____

_____

_____

Challenge:

Build a model of two numbers and share it with a partner. Solve your partner's problem.
Draw your partner's problem and solution.

_____

_____

_____

Assessment:

1. Model 26 studs. Show how to subtract 17 from this amount by decomposing the 26.

Write a math sentence for this problem. _____

Draw your solution.

2. Build a model of the problem: 34 − 16 = ☐

Show all the steps. Draw your solution.

3. Build a model that shows the decomposing process for 23 – 14. Draw your model. Solve the problem and explain your work.

_____

_____

_____

RESULT UNKNOWN PROBLEMS WITHIN 20

Part 1

Problem #1: $7 - 3 = \boxed{}$

The missing number is called the _____.

Build either the 1x10 strips or a ten-frame model to show how to solve the problem. Show all parts of the model. Draw your model and label it. Explain how you found the solution.

○○○○○○○○○○○○○○○○○○○
○○○○○○○○○○○○○○○○○○○
○○○○○○○○○○○○○○○○○○○
○○○○○○○○○○○○○○○○○○○
○○○○○○○○○○○○○○○○○○○
○○○○○○○○○○○○○○○○○○○
○○○○○○○○○○○○○○○○○○○
○○○○○○○○○○○○○○○○○○○
○○○○○○○○○○○○○○○○○○○
○○○○○○○○○○○○○○○○○○○
○○○○○○○○○○○○○○○○○○○
○○○○○○○○○○○○○○○○○○○
○○○○○○○○○○○○○○○○○○○

_____

_____

_____

Problem #2: 9 − 5 = ☐

The missing number is called the _____.

Build either the 1x10 strips or a ten-frame model to show how to solve the problem. Show all parts of the model. Draw your model and label it. Explain how you found the solution.

_____

_____

_____

Problem #3: 8 – 2 = ☐

Build either the 1x10 strips or a ten-frame model to show how to solve the problem. Show all parts of the model. Draw your model and label it. Explain how you found the solution.

Part 2

1. Can you build a model that shows this math sentence? $5 - 3 = \boxed{}$

You can use a 1x10 strip model or a ten-frame model. Draw your model.

Draw all three parts of the problem. Label the *minuend*, *subtrahend*, and *difference*. Explain how you found the missing term.

2. Can you build a model that shows this math sentence? 10 – 7 = ☐

You can use a 1x10 strip model or a ten-frame model. Draw your model.

Draw all three parts of the problem. Label the *minuend*, *subtrahend*, and *difference*. Explain how you found the missing term.

_____

_____

_____

3. Can you build a model that shows this math sentence? 6 − 3 = ☐

You can use a 1x10 strip model or a ten-frame model. Draw your model.

Draw all three parts of the problem. Label the *minuend*, *subtrahend*, and *difference*. Explain how you found the missing term.

_____

_____

_____

Challenge:

Can you build a model that shows this math sentence? 12 − 7 = ☐ *Hint*: Use two 1x10 strips or two ten-frames to model the number 12.

Draw your solution model. Explain your solution.

_____

_____

_____

Assessment:

1. Build a model that shows the solution to this problem: $15 - 6 =$ ☐

Draw your model and label the parts of the problem.

2. Build a ten-frame model of 20. Draw your model. Show how to subtract 3. Show the result unknown number.

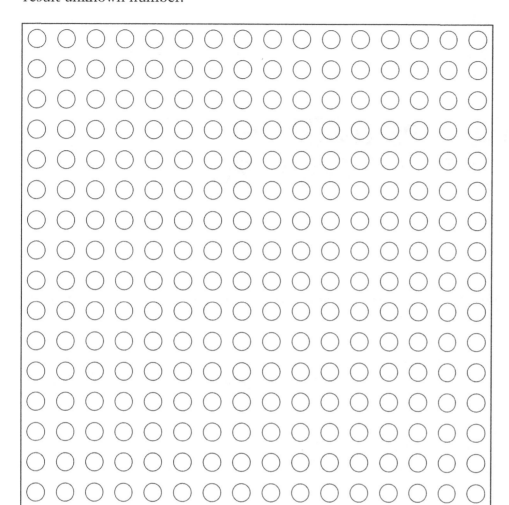

3. Circle the math sentences that are NOT correct. Build models if you need help.

16 – 5 = 11   14 – 9 = 6

15 – 6 = 8   11 – 3 = 8

4. What would be the correct solution for each problem that is not correct? How do you know?

_____

_____

_____

CHANGE UNKNOWN PROBLEMS WITHIN 20

Part 1

Problem #1: $7 - \boxed{} = 4$

Build either three 1x10 strips or a ten-frame model to show how to solve the problem. Show all parts of the model. Draw your model.

What is the answer to the subtraction problem (the change number)?_____

Label the *minuend*, *subtrahend* and *difference*.

Which term tells the amount the start number is changed by?_____

Problem #2: $9 - \boxed{} = 5$

Build either three 1x10 strips or a ten-frame model to show how to solve the problem. Show all parts of the model. Draw your model.

What is the answer to the subtraction problem (the change number)?_____

Label the *minuend*, *subtrahend* and *difference*.

Which term tells the amount the start number is changed by?_____

Problem #3: $8 - \boxed{} = 2$

Build either three 1x10 strips or a ten-frame model to show how to solve the problem. Show all parts of the model. Draw your model.

What is the answer to the subtraction problem (the change number)?_____

Label the *minuend*, *subtrahend* and *difference*.

Which term tells the amount the start number is changed by?_____

Part 2

1. Can you build a model that shows this math sentence? $5 - \boxed{} = 3$

You can use a 1x10 strip model or a ten-frame model. Draw your model.

Draw all three parts of the problem. Label the *minuend*, *subtrahend*, and *difference*. Explain how you found the missing term.

_____

_____

_____

2. Can you build a model that shows this math sentence? $10 - \boxed{} = 4$

You can use a 1x10 strip model or a ten-frame model. Draw your model.

Draw all three parts of the problem. Label the *minuend, subtrahend,* and *difference*. Explain how you found the missing term.

_____

_____

_____

3. Can you build a model that shows this math sentence? $7 - \boxed{} = 5$

You can use a 1x10 strip model or a ten-frame model. Draw your model.

Draw all three parts of the problem. Label the *minuend*, *subtrahend*, and *difference*. Explain how you found the missing term.

_____

_____

_____

Challenge:

Can you build a model to show this problem? $12 - \boxed{} = 7$

Draw your solution model that shows the change unknown number. Explain your solution.

_____

_____

_____

Assessment:

1. Label each number in the following problem using words from the word bank.

Word Bank:
    Subtrahend
    Minuend
    Change Unknown Number
    Difference

$12 - 5 = 7$

12 is the _____

5 is the _____

7 is the _____

2. Label each number in the following problem using words from the word bank.

Word Bank:
    Subtrahend
    Minuend
    Change Unknown Number
    Difference

$10 - 2 = 8$

10 is the _____

2 is the _____

8 is the _____

3. Build a model using bricks to solve: $9 - \boxed{} = 3$

Show all the steps. Draw your model and label it. Explain how you know what the change number is.

[grid of circles representing a LEGO baseplate]

_____

_____

_____

START UNKNOWN PROBLEMS WITHIN 20

Part 1

1. ☐ – 3 = 7

How can you find the missing number (*minuend*) that belongs in the box?

_____

_____

_____

Build three 1x10 strips or three ten-frames.

The left strip or ten-frame represents the _____.

The center strip or ten-frame represents the _____.

The right strip or ten-frame represents the _____.

Draw your model.

2. To show the problem, how many studs should be placed on the left strip? _____

How many studs should be placed on the center strip? _____

How many studs should be placed on the right strip? _____

The left strip represents the _____
number. It will be the largest number in the problem.

Model the problem and draw your model above. Write the math sentence your model represents now.

_____

3. Take all the studs from the right strip and all the studs from the center strip and place them on the left strip. How many studs are on the left strip now? _____

Draw your model.

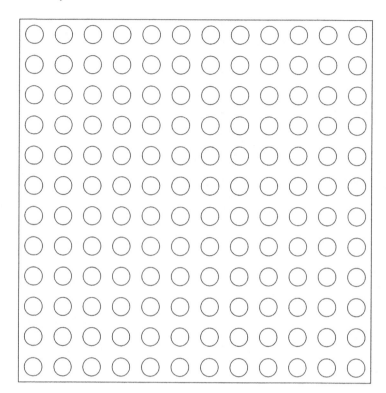

4. Check your model by moving studs back to their original strips.

5. Model all three parts of the problem. Draw and label your model. Write the complete math sentence.

6. ☐ – 6 = 3

Build three 1x10 strips or three ten-frames. Place studs on each strip or ten-frame to model the problem. Draw your model. Write the math sentence your model represents now.

_____

7. The _____ number is missing. How can you find the missing number?

_____

_____

_____

8. Combine the strips to get the solution. What is the solution? _____

9. Work backward on your model to make sure your answer is correct.

10. Place bricks on your model to show the *minuend, subtrahend,* and *difference*. Draw this model, label each part of the problem, and explain how you know the start number is 9.

_____

_____

_____

Part 2

1. Can you build a model that shows this math sentence? $\boxed{} - 4 = 1$

You can use a 1x10 strip model or a ten-frame model. Draw your model.

Solve the problem and show all three numbers in the problem on your model. Draw this model and explain how you found the minuend.

_____

_____

_____

2. Can you build a model that shows this math sentence? ☐ − 5 = 3

You can use a 1x10 strip model or a ten-frame model. Draw your model.

Solve the problem and show all three numbers in the problem on your model. Draw this model and explain how you found the minuend.

_____

_____

_____

3. Can you build a model that shows this math sentence? $\boxed{} - 4 = 2$

You can use a 1x10 strip model or a ten-frame model. Draw your model.

Solve the problem and show all three numbers in the problem on your model. Draw this model and explain how you found the minuend.

(A 12 × 10 grid of circles representing LEGO brick studs)

_____

_____

_____

Challenge:

Create a problem for a partner to solve. Check to make sure your partner goes through all the steps. Discuss your solutions.

Assessment:

1. Model this problem: ☐ – 7 = 2

Show all the steps to prove your solution. Draw your models.

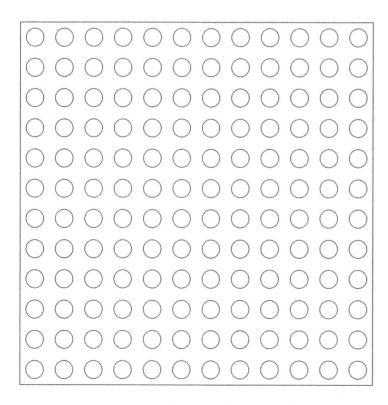

2. Build a model that shows a solution to a problem where the difference in the problem is 5. Draw your model. Circle the start number. Write the math sentence for your problem.

_____

3. Model this problem: ☐ – 2 = 5

Model the solution and draw it. Circle the start number. Write the math sentence for your problem.

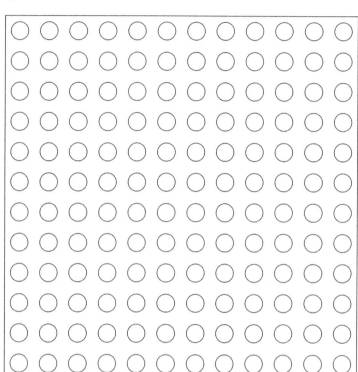

---

4. Circle the start numbers in these problems:

6 – 4 = 2

12 – 5 = 7

22 – 16 = 6

SUBTRACTION
Student Assessment Chart

Name _____

Performance Skill	Not yet	With help	On target	Comments
I can model the subtraction of two numbers and label all the parts of a subtraction problem.				
I can show and tell what it means to subtract numbers using the correct words.				
I can subtract within 20.				
I can model how to find the first missing number (start unknown) in a subtraction problem.				
I can model how to find the second missing number (change unknown) in a subtraction problem.				
I can model how to find the missing result in a subtraction problem.				
I can decompose numbers to make sets of tens and ones.				

Made in the USA
Coppell, TX
31 May 2023

17526598R00044